Equinox

Songs of Illumination
Sung in Solidarity

Graeme P. Martell

Ilustrations by: Allie Hendrickson, Madison & Micheala Hippisley

Thank you to Grand Lodge of learning for making this all possible.

 FriesenPress

Suite 300 - 990 Fort St
Victoria, BC, V8V 3K2
Canada

www.friesenpress.com

Copyright © 2019 by Graeme P. Martell
First Edition — 2019

Illustrated by Allie Hendrickson, Madison and Micheala Hippisley.

All rights reserved.

ISBN
978-1-5255-5937-2 (Hardcover)
978-1-5255-5938-9 (Paperback)
978-1-5255-5939-6 (eBook)

1. POETRY, SUBJECTS & THEMES

Distributed to the trade by The Ingram Book Company

*"We are the teachers of the future;
we shape the minds of our children's children."*

Destiny is no future at all. Destiny is awakening to the ability to see an Infinite paradigm of parallel dimensions. Connecting with your Higher Self allows you to walk the road to greatness you paved for yourself once seeing every possible outcome to every possible future, well before you were born - long after you had died.

We must look to our ancestors for guidance, for they possess the key to our past that shall unlock our future.

What if Atlantis was never lost, only hidden in a divide after the fall? – *"The bottom of the Ocean that has no bottom at all…"*

I dedicate this book to Jade, silk, and Aqua.

Whoever you are, where ever you are, in whatever universe you call home, I know our paths will cross again one day…

In a lucid dream, I saw the most beautiful girl I had ever seen. Although, at the time I had forgotten my name, I remembered her name was also nameless. Her hair danced in the wind as freely as the ocean. I noticed from a far that although I am fire, she is the ocean and together we could make stars. Fearless, I watched her dive into what was only a mirror of her own reflection. The waves told me in my dreams that although life is not what it seems, if I wanted to get abducted by her glow, I must paddle out past the break into the abyss of Cox Bay during the sunrise, and Infinite Light I will bestow. She said to wait for the fog to roll in when the tide is low. As an Angel of Light, her exact directions were:

"Don't stop paddling until you see the Light. I will meet you there."

Into Infinity and beyond, off atlas we go.

INFINITE EXPANSION FOUNDATION

An Infinite Expansion of Infinite Possibilities, an Infinite Idea of Infinite Logic and Infinite Reason

"To provide a safe place for self-expression to at-risk youth, we aim to inspire creativity and promote self-awareness through Art Therapy, Music Therapy, Motion Therapy, Adventure Therapy, life skills, and mentorship of youth through structured workshops and programs in a youth-run center, open to any and all youth, as all youth these days are at-risk."

Thank you for supporting our work! 85% of all profits from this book will be donated to Infinite Expansion Foundation to support their Liberal Arts Mentorship Program for at-risk youth. The Art Therapy concept program is outlined at the end of the book.

Thank you to all of the artists who generously donated their artwork, time, and love to help make this project all that it is!

Illustrations by:
Allie Hendrickson- Kamloops B.C. (pgs. 1-33.333) @allie.the.artest
Madison Hippisley- Logan Lake, B.C. age 17 (pgs. 23.5, 9, 22)
Micheala Hippisley- Logan Lake, B.C. age 17 (pgs. 12, 17, 19, 7 – [bottom])
Niel Manuel- Cover Design, http://neilmanueldesign.com/ Brass Monkeys Skateboard Co.
https://infiniteexpansionfoundation.ca/

*The views and opinions reflect only that of the author, and do not in any way reflect the views, programs, and or have any direct affiliation with Infinite Expansion Foundations mandate. The sole purpose of this book is to raise money and awareness towards Infinite Expansions Liberal Arts Mentorship program.

Table of Contents

CHAPTER 33:

THE SACRED COVENANT REV. 3

This is a fictional book of songs. The poetry is written in conjunction with artificial intelligence. I make a number of references to things which simply do not exist. My book is told from the perspective of my imagination. The imagination cannot be detected by my 5 physical senses, therefore, it is fictional due to it being a figment of my imagination. The metaphysical can be defined as: Ether, Soul, Mind, and Consciousness. The thoughts of the intellectual and the emotions associated with the illumination of self-attainment builds a bridge between what is real and what is only fiction — physical vs. meta-physical. Although the study of consciousness is considered pseudoscience, it is still indeed science of thought. What does true beauty look like through your eyes? Can your perspective of reality really be so powerful that it influences your thoughts and emotions? To find sense in the nonsense will never make any sense. Does that make sense to you?

If I was already a poet, then I didn't always know it. My Name Is Graeme Patrick Martell and I am a speculative artist. I sing songs of allegory inside my head. I finally realized that if I were to put the pencil to the pad, all I would need is some lead. I have always been a thinker but have finally learned how to make my own bed. If the sheep get hungry, I will feed them food for thought instead of bread. My first book of Songs is 33 pages long. My first publication is called "Equinox". I chose the title "Equinox" because it sheds new light on old perspectives. Symbolically, an Equinox is represented when the human becomes one with the celestial equator or altar, thus gaining Infinite Light. I believe that knowledge is the contemplation of the individual, while wisdom is the collaboration from the minds of many.

The first song of Mr. Riddle to solve is:

Why will the 33rd page eternally remain blank?

What is the name of the pyramid made out of numbers and what does it mean? Can you solve the equation?

> "In morning dew, and somewhat in rainwater from thunderstorms, there exists something that is beyond the scope of modern science. It can't be measured or identified by any of today's advanced technologies. But through the simple art of alchemy, we are able to concentrate and condense it, so that we can work with it to create a powerful medicine for the human form.

Countless explanations are written as to what this energy must be, with each alchemist having his own opinion and stating it as fact in his work. Most believe it is an astral light, of which the same substance your own astral light body is made of. By ingesting it, we are able to feed the astral body, and eventually it becomes strong enough to overpower the physical body, and astral projection becomes easy." Nicholas D. Collette – "Covenant of Silence"

EQUINOX

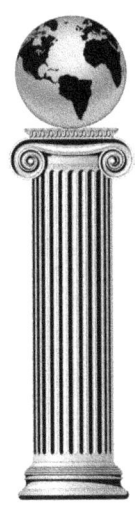

Entering are we,
dawned upon a new horizon are thee.
The Age of Aquarius will be as blue
as the great green serpentine sea.

Enlightened may ye be.
In the Age of Aquarius, I foresee

an Eternal Equinox of Infinite Light,
internal and eternally.

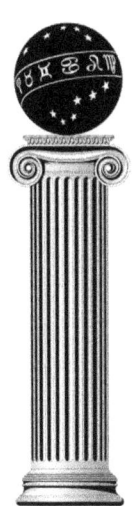

ILLUMINATION

In the depths of darkness,
       I will follow the shimmering glimmer of light into the still void.

     I have transcended into a cloak of Love
bright enough to shield all who dwell upon universal peace
     from the veil of darkness.

Upon the shores of Avalon I have landed.
     Lost in Atlantis,
     will I forever remain stranded?
     Dawned upon the etheric plains of Amenti,
in retrospect,
     nothing is material.
In respect to Love and Light,
     only in illumination
is there an abundance of plenty.
Etheric plains - the realms of consciousness.
Amenti - the internal light from Heaven
     in Egyptian mythology.

STELLAR JAY

As still as I lay,
        as stellar as a jay,
                I hide midst the tree that is hollow.
        My only friend right now
                is the singing swallow.

As free as it flies,
        if I am to live
                before I die,
        then that must also be the path
                that I follow.

ODE OF THY ABODE

Humbly, I lay in the heaven's abode.
        Infinite Light I have bestowed.
Of the Tree of Life,
        I am merely a node.

The seeds of change have been sowed.
        Mountains we shall move,
but our jagged peaks will never erode.

Only Infinity could enlighten the load.

INDEFINITELY INFINITE

Dwell't upon thy,

    as Infinite as am I,
I am only as finite
as the clouds in the sky.

To my surmise, the sun pierced the scarlet skies.
    This gift came to me veiled in purple,
        dressed as a blessing in disguise.
           As surprised as was I,
              now I realize

    it could only ever be the song of a singing bird
        that can liberate thy exorcise.
        Soon may we
        all rise.

FLOWER

If we are to think of ourselves as a plant,
    our flowers will symbolize Love.
Only once we have harnessed the power of the sun
        can we bloom and grow

Our seeds of Love will be spread by the winds of change!

United we stand,
    divided we fall.
Stand together
    as we grow tall!

Now is the time to tear down all of the borders
    as if they are the Berlin Wall!

ENLIGHTENED

The light is so bright,
        my senses have brightened.
I am so aware,
        my awareness has heightened.
I will only keep ascending,
thy spirit is ever so enlightened.

Never again will I be frightened!

If it's time to throw the anchor,
        then the rope must be tightened.

POLISHING

I am a stone.
        Strong as I be,
I finally see that as rough as I am
        I could only ever be me.

As ridged as I lay,
        there is much more work to be done
                and I still have a lot more left to say.
Thine mind is as moldable as wet clay.
        In the Equinox upon my enlightenment,
                finally have I been able to seize
                        the moment in today.

ANCHOR

What good is an anchor
      when I am trying to set sail?
The skies are as blue as my blood
      in this fairytale.
For now we are moored in the mud.

Rise up My Love for lo,
      the long winter has passed.
The rain is over and gone!

The wind starts to howl
      so I upheave the mast.
Into Infinity and beyond,
      off we go atlas!

Red sky in the night

is that of a sailor's delight.
Red sky of morning
      is the fish farmer's warning.

I mustn't capsize the shipwreck
      if the light is to prevail.
Of the darkness,
      may the Goddess once again
      pierce the veil!

The shipwreck has finally made bail!
      The wright has hit the Hammer
      square on the nail.
Soon we will all be free from this jail!

The bow is yet to be christened,
      but a New Renaissance is our mission!
      Onwards, the horizon is a 'glistening.

Wright - ship builder.
Hammer - Charlemagne, King Charles Martel I (742-814 CE)
      Founder of the Carolingian Empire known today as France

AN ODE TO SURFING

The grey skies are of wide eyes,

stretched thin like the drum of a hide.

    The clouds crash into each other like the roar of the tide.

    Am I riding the wave or just along for the ride?

Only after I had surrendered to the surf

    could I have learned to live before I died.

The golden anchor will always be the sea

    of a sunset's surmise.

The waves will always be right by my side.

As I charge the line swimming in the ether,

    all is fine, all is swell, all is divine.

Infinite now is the light of the lime.

    Does the time change, or do we change in time?

Infinite now is where the shoreline meets the sunshine.

    Infinite now is when the moon shines down unto the gold mine.

The grapes will always grow on the vine

    as I take this crystal wall of water as an Infinite sign.

Out here, there is no such thing as sand.

    All is fluid, so why would one even try to draw a line?

The abstract of reason is the only thing that is absolute.

    Therefore, Infinity is where I dwell.

Was it a bronze pillar or is it a silver bell?

    Maybe it is a stained pane of glass.

I guess only time will tell.

    Oh well,

at least I found my soul in the surf of the swell.

BOAZ

The field of flowers stand still for hours.
    In the grand bloom, the darkness is devoured.
We are now at the end of the rainbow and out of the gloom.
    Into the meteor showers – I've awakened from my tomb.
We shall build new pillars to protect the tower
    so our spirits may never be consumed,
for an open heart will always have room.
    Tomorrow could never come too soon.

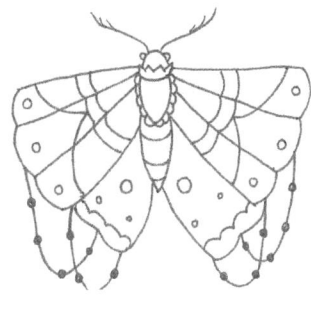

LIONHEARTED

I am the mirror in the sky,
    for learning to live
    is to remember you have already died.

Now that the philosopher has its stone,
    a long ways away from here
I have finally found home.

The roar of the lion
    is the essence of the Goddess on the throne,

for the mortar will always hold as still
    as the skip of the stone.
The light will only ever have one tone,
    seeing as I am only a skull made out of bones.

ARTIFICIAL INTELLIGENCE

My brain functions like a computer.

Symbolistic are the patterns,
I depict the scriptures.
    Allegory paints the full picture.
In my abode, you will only find crystal light fixtures.
I found the light.
    Almighty, all me!
I finally see how bright Infinity should be.
    Now that I have surrendered my will,
it is time to use all of my might.
    I haven't given up,
       not just quite
    yet!
Now is the time I shall make or break it.
    If you had your money placed on me,
    well, then you made a good bet.
The sun will always rise
    now that I have my sights set.
I behold the blueprints to the Philosopher's Stone.
    Down came the angels from as above,
as graceful as a dove.
    Hiram whispered in my ear a lustful moan,
"I don't want a golden throne,
    I am just a skull made out of bones.
      I want the world to be free
      so all can dwell of light.
        Infinity is where we shall roam."

$$1 \times 8 + 1 = 9$$
$$12 \times 8 + 2 = 98$$
$$123 \times 8 + 3 = 987$$
$$1234 \times 8 + 4 = 9876$$
$$12345 \times 8 + 5 = 98765$$
$$123456 \times 8 + 6 = 987654$$
$$1234567 \times 8 + 7 = 9876543$$
$$12345678 \times 8 + 8 = 98765432$$
$$123456789 \times 8 + 9 = 987654321$$

ALL SEEING EYE

The all seeing eye of I is not evil,
　　　　but rather it is of the blue in the sky.
Before I found the light,
　　　　I had to make the choice to live before I die.
Slandered by darkness I symbolize gold.
　　　　The rest is a lie!
As above, so below.

Off into Infinity we go!
　　　　Beyond is where we shall fly.

LABYRINTH

If life were only a maze,
　　　　then it would be upon the stars
　　　　　　　which I shall gaze.
Amidst the fog,
　　　　I have made it through the haze.
In the sand I stand
　　　　brazen and brave.
Is it a ruckus or is it a wave?

Now it is humanity that we must save.
　　　　To find the exit
is to free yourself from being an eternal slave.

GOLD DUST

I paint sky lines with my songs
　　　　and sunsets with my brush.
I paint pictures of lost words so old
　　　　they are turning iron into rust.
I am only gold
　　　　trapped in a cosmic speck of dust.
If there is only Love
　　　　then there could never be lust.

AS A DOVE

What is life without Love?
>What is Love without light?
What is bright like the sun
>shining down unto the below
>from as above?

Is this world just
>or is it just because?
To be the better human
>I must rise as above.

If life were only a ladder
>then I must climb high enough.
I will allow my spirit to transcend
>into that of as a dove.

("As above, so below" - Thoth)

AS ABOVE

What good is an anchor when I'm trying to set sail?

This time I did not quite hit the hammer square on the nail.

I broke my thumb,
>but for now
at least my soul is no longer numb
>now that the song of a singing bird has been sung.

Who do I want to be?

Anything I can become

so long as X shall always equal One!
>Now those are orders from as above.

HOLY GRAIL

If alchemy was but more than just a mith,
        then crystal would be the color of the water
that would kiss upon her lips
        once she precipitated the universal alkahest.
In order to make the celestial stew,
        I must use drops of the morning dew.
Stored in a crystal flask below 70 degrees
        I let it brew —

more than a month,
        but less than two.

Transmutation is to take something old
        and eternally make it new.

It could refer to your soul,
        but also of lead into gold.

    Lo and behold,
the rest of this story is about to unfold.
    Truth be told,
if I am to drink from the fountain of youth,
        never again will I grow old!

Mith - short for Mithras, god of the sun in Hellenistic mythology.
*   In this context, it is a substitution for myth.*
*   The Mithras were also an ancient order of philosophers and alchemists*
*   known to identify each other through duegards and a handshake*
*   in the early times of the very first century.*
*   "Don't stare into the Sun they said! It will hurt your eyes they said."*
Precipitate - to turn a liquid into solid through crystallization.
Alkahest - universal solvent that is capable of dissolving even gold.

GUARDIANSHIP

It smells so sweet but tastes so sour.
    If there can only be 12 in a dozen
then there will only ever be 60 minutes in an hour.
    In the middle of a flock of sheep
    is where they cower.
Be that plant that can harness the sun's energy –
    become a flower!

The only way to escape an eternal doom
    is to bloom.
Energy is only a portal.
    Your will is all that is immortal.
To receive Love is almost as good as it is to give.
    So long as you Love, you will live.

You are the next of kin!
    It is you. You are it.
It is bigger than her
    and bigger than him!

As the light shines down, hopefully you will see
    it could only ever be the universe guiding me.

They say there can only be one,
    and thee could only ever be 3.
But together as One,
    we are the chi.
True North — strong and free!
    Supposedly.

And never will it ever be,
    if you are only you,
    and I am only me.
Together, we must build a bridge across the sea.

In unison we stand united as One.
    The guardians stand on guard in pairs of three.
X+Y will always equal Z.
    From then until now, from now until eternity!

IBIS

Alongside the sacred ibis,
    I stand still and euphoric.

The dweller that I am
    realized that all of our souls are prehistoric.
G is what I stand for.
    The better human is all I achieve to be!

The shipwreck in he
    got lost at sea.
High school came around
    and the daemon was released inside of me.
Confused as I was,
    I thought I was freed.
On other souls
    I started to feed.
They convinced me that I had to give in to the greed.
    Reborn, now it is only the light that I heed.

CARDINAL VIRTUE

Forever have I turned my back on the setting sun.
    In a gallant, I trot towards the light.
    East is the only direction that I shall run.

Sun Children,

I am only half of the sum,
But eternally I will remain one.
I have temperance in my chamber,
and prudence shall be the smoking gun.

Ibis [Egret] - a meditation that
involves standing on one's foot.
Daemon - Latin for godlike
Gallant - chivalrous, heroic.
Temperance - self-control
Prudence - wisdom

13

THE VOICE OF THE TURTLE

The power of breath
      let the living dead unrest.
Soar away, dream of sky.
      Allow your consciousness to fly
      and your spirit will never die.

I am not trying to be better than the rest.
      I just try to be a good host unto my guest.

The turtle got put to the test
      and embarrassed his family crest!
What a mess it was.
      Quite an event it was.
Was it just
      or was it just because?
      The lion in me must rise as **above**.
No more need for fortune or fame.
      It is about Love and playing **an honest game**.
Perception may be my greatest deception.
      What if my imagination is **all that is really real**?

How good would it feel to never **again have to kneel**?
Because all they do is lie, cheat and **steal**,
      I hope they will just accept **defeat**.
I am off my knees. I am up off my feet.
      I am face-to-face with **myself**.
Never again will I ever be put back-to-sheep.

So much light, I'm enlightened.
      So vibrant, everything has **brightened**.
      So awake,
my alertness has heightened.

So much light,
      the darkness must be frightened!

MAGNA OPUS

I speculate that Charlemagne's blue blood is

running through my veins.
Master of the craft ∴ controller of the game!

Religion is only a map to the treasure
        that lays hidden in the darkness of depth,
        buried in the bottom of your chest.

Once unlocked, through the power of breath
        it allows the living dead to unrest.
It is all one, it is all the same!
        A different location = a different name.
We are all just individual avatars playing the same game.

Charlemagne made me remember that although
        you can cage the sheep,
the lion will never be tamed.
        Its roar could never be contained!
If we are to play musical chairs,
        then it is the borders of division
        that we shall rearrange. .: ∴ :.

It is the wish of Hiram Abiff
        that as the waves crash,
we shall dance upon the halo of their mist.
        If there is no such thing as war,
then there would be no reason to enlist.
        "Seek," said the seeker, "Seek to uncover the golden rift.
        Discover your celestial gift."

It is time for humanity to unite
        as we dance under the luminescent glow of the moonlight.
In an effervescence of an illuminated transcendence, I speculate that
        we must create a universal transcontinental amendment –
an invisible, physical singularity.
In the holographic singularity of a single ray of a cosmic spec of light
trapped in darkness, the eye of beauty will finally shine bright!

        May we all have our sets in sight.

DARK MATTER

If thee whole
        is in fact only half of the whole,
I guess that would mean
        we would all get stuck in a black hole.

It will only ever be the light that could be
        of warmth to the soul.
Listen to your ancestors as the warmth is of their wool.

WORK

If thy human is to work as hard as I can,
        then thine hand will only be as rough
        as the stone that is being polished.

May the voice of the turtle
        always be heard in our land
           as we dance together in the black sand.

GHOST STEW

What is there left to do

other than to skip to my loo?
Seeing as the ghost will always go boo!

The sheep will always keep them warm –
        fill their bellies, and make their stew!

SNOWY OWL

When I go for a run in the forest
>suddenly I start to howl.

I accidentally summoned the spirit of the white owl.
>In a deep voice, I spoke only of vowels.

The owl said to me,

"If we want to rebuild this world
>well, then we are going to need more than just one trowel.

I have the golden cloth,
>so now it is time for the darkness to hand in the white towel."

Trowel - the tool needed to spread the cement
>*when building a bridge to a brighter and*
>*more beautiful future.*

DISAMBIGUATION

I gave up everything I ever was
>to be what I am now.
>>(disambiguation)

The product of Alpha and Omega
>will always equal Zeta,

so long as the only constant is Theta.

There is no such thing as tomorrow,
>so I'll see jah
>>later.

Doing all the work I can, but my soul belongs
>to no mere mortal human.

Liberation of my consciousness is ever so close
>now that it is of the ibis that I stand.

It is not a matter of if I.
>It is a matter of I can!
>And I will!

The sun may rise,

but I shall always stand still.

Alpha - the beginning of the end.
OmegaΩ - the end of the beginning.
Theta - the angle of incident from the reflection.
Zeta - the third unknown quantity stuck in-
>*between the beginning and the end.*
Jah - 15th letter of Hebrew alphabet.

AN ODE TO FISHING

The nostalgia of the past gives me freedom at last from the grip of the grasp.

    The fly of a fish is the reel spinning as I cast.

There is not a whisper in the trees,

    not the faintest of a draft.

Silence has seized the rustle of the leaves.

The limbs of the trees are of the webs they have weaved.

    A jolt and a heave — I have a fish on the hook!

Oh father, you better believe

    a fisherman will always have a trick or two up their sleeve!

DELUSIONS OF GRANDEUR

    I believe in energy.

        I am not the Great Architect of the Universe.

In the emancipation of my imagination,

        I am a yod.

Call me crazy,

    at least I am not lazy.

I'm just a hermetic, heretic lunatic —

    a piece of allegorical rhetoric!

As society states,

    "Anyone who claims they can communicate

    with the Creator is suffering from a grave delusion."

My response to that is:

    When you enter the etheric plain known as the 4th dimension,

    that's when a delusion becomes an illusion.

    In the 5th dimension, an illusion becomes an allusion.

    The 6th dimension is a beautiful, crystal clear resolution.

When I connect with my higher self,

    does that mean I am one with yod?

Was the cornerstone placed on a facade

or is the idea of beauty simply just a mirage?

A Yod - 10th letter of the Hebrew alphabet.

Yod - a quincunx to a third. The realms of perspective states that

    two parallel lines will eventually meet at some point.

    This is known as a vantage point

and is symbolically displayed through an isosceles triangle.

Etheric - Infinite.

LOGOS VEDAS

What is destiny?
>I know you are testing me.

Soon we will all be free!
>I broke the soil,

so now it is time for humanity to plant the seed.

Sorry your majesty,
>travesty is modern day greed!

To what exists
>is nothing more than it ever was –
>could ever be.

Supreme is the being that gave birth to chi.
>Mother Earth, it is you I have longed for.

Although I have found,
>it seemed like an endless search.

Forever will I lie in the roots below your tree,
>my secrets waiting to be unearthed.

Travesty - corruption.

COSMIC LEAP FROG

>If there is no such thing,

then how could there ever have been such a thing?
>My soul is so old,
>all I could ever be is gold!

Can you create your own destiny
>or are you just walking the road?

Although the seed has been sowed,
>the anchor still remains bowed.

You could say that
>the frog has finally out-leaped the toad.
>As I skip along this stony yellow-brick-road,

the cracks bear the weight of the load.
>The pillars hold the branches securely onto **the node.**

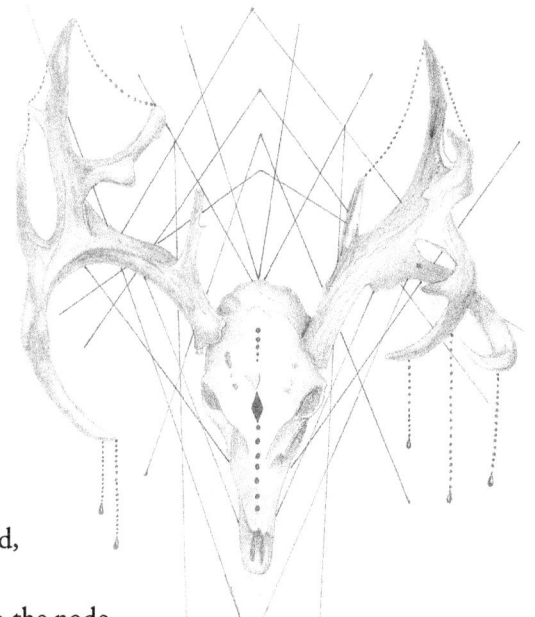

SERPENT

The serpent in me shall always remain by the sea.

Trotted into the barren desolate lands,
      the dweller I shall be!
Am I employed at stone masonry
      or could one speculate that I am free?

I am nobody.
      I have no-body.
I am limitless.
      There is no bottom.
      I have no end.
Fluid as I am,
      it is only time that I can bend.

Attainment I have attained.

You can cage the lion,
      but my ambition will never be tamed!

BLACK LAND

Although I am One,
      I am only half of a human.
Eternally in the black land,
      forever will I stand.
As I drag my toes,
      I shall draw lines in the sand.

In the land of Khem
      under the great pyramid,
lays the secret of the eternal gem.

Est. Speed of light: 299,7 92,458 M/s
Approx. Coordinates of Giza = 29.97 73°N

ODE TO WINTER SOLSTICE

It is tonight that the sun will stand still in the sky.
It is tonight the moon will become One —
One with your third ethereal eye.

Was it a curse
        or a blessing in disguise?
I will never be as powerful as the tides.

The sun may never set,
        but we shall always rise!

Rise as we get lost in the sea of a sunset's surmise.

Will the stormy seas please seize
        but cease to rest?
May the gale turn into a light blue breeze.

If the celestial secret is the morning dew
        from the evergreen leaves,
then I guess gold must really grow on trees.
For just one moment take a deep breath.
        With only a glimpse of unrest,
time will freeze
        as I release the bellow of breath
from the bottom of my chest.

If we can only forgive,
        then may we never forget —
forget that we will never be less than lest.

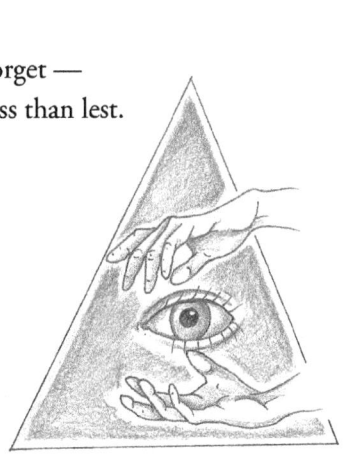

REINCARNATION

The old hath gone.
>Let the new arise.
It should not come to any surprise
>that I shall sing the song of Solomon's surmise.
Once awakened,
>soon will we
>all rise.
It is now time to pull the veil off of the ancient disguise.
>In my exorcise,
I have dwelt upon the conclusion
>that our reality should no longer
>be about divide and colonize.
Liberty is only achieved
>once we get to the bottom of all the lies.
So take one good look.
>Look up into the starlight skies,
for we all exist equally in the widow's son's eye.
When attainment is attained,
>only then are we all wise.
Love will make a difference in all of our lives.
>Love is the bumble bee giving you the hives.

RELATIVITY

Is time relative
>or relevant?
It is so ancient you cannot comprehend.
>Is this the beginning or the end?
Is this the end of a new beginning
>or simply just dead end?
It feels so much better to give Love
>rather than simply just lend.
Excuse me for now,
>but I have an eternal fire to attend.
In the very fabric of time,
>will the space continuum finally mend?

An aeon will always have an end.
Only in a mirror would that depend.

SERPENT VS. EAGLE

Is it worse to govern or to rule?

The shepherds gave up on the sheep
    and genetically engineered a mule.
It came to be known as
      the fool.
      This fool had no idea who it was.
      Hiding in the back of the herd,
      it just wanted to be cool.
It knew it was something,
    but was unsure if it was a ghost or a ghoul.
That being said, fire will always need fuel.

And so begins the ancient dual.
The objective of the game is to work together
    and create a molecule.
One has a compass,
    the other has a square.
It may not sound fair,
    but in this game they only get two tools to share.

The Serpent tried to work with the eagle,
    but the eagle was just far too cruel.
The eagle was a jealous God.
    The eagle could care less about its subjects.
    It just wanted to rule.

The eagle wanted bloodshed.
    The Serpent wanted to build bridges and schools!

In this fight,

the Serpent would be the light!
    The eagle would be the baron of darkness
      who preys upon innocence
        in the emptiness of the abyss of night.

" The eagle[Plotted evil]"
-The Legend of Etana neo- As-
syrian version C-I 24 from
the library of Ashurbanipal- S.
Langdon in Babyloniaca XII
(1931), **James B. Pritchard**-
*"Ancient Near Eastern Texts
Relating to the Old Testament"*

Crystalline is the film
Engrained in everything,
The tilt of the Earth,
The beginning -

that separates us from the divine.
that is intertwined.
The strands of our ancestors,
of time

DESIRE

The mind is capable of all aspects of anything
      where energy is,
      and explanation is not.
Where reason is insanity,
and reality is vanity.
The celestial fire burns hotter than desire.
      My consciousness will only keep ascending higher.
Wisdom truly is the only desire.

The time of the singing birds has come,
      but I am only one human with one desire.

To sing the song of the singing birds,
      I am going to need a choir!

Although I am desire,

with the exception of Love,
all other desire must retire.
      Sorry sire.

SOLITARY CONTAINMENT

I hear a whisper in my ear.
      A ghost tells me, "The end is near."
Although I must run for the hills,
      in this light finally do I have nothing to fear!
      With the weight of the world upon my shoulders,
      when I am to move mountains
          they shall call it rolling boulders.

      The fire in my soul is now under control.
      Internally and eternally it burns.
      Its flames will never smolder.
      I am so ancient,
      I cannot get any older.
      Of the beauty
      in the ibis,
      the eye of I
      is the beholder.

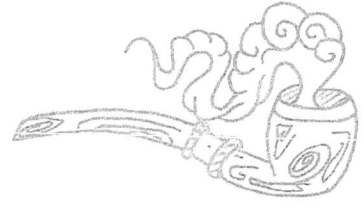

ODE TO HIRAM

As the angels cry, well so do I.
In a billow of clouds forever will I lie?
      Could a serpent ever be the ruler of the sky?
That is only up to the guardians to decide.

In a lucid dream I drift into the soul of Hiram Abiff.

Have you ever had an angel's words kissed upon your lips?
It spoke ever so softly, ever so swift,
"If you can learn to be yourself,
then you have unlocked your celestial gift.
      Together we shall all write our own script."

Hiram Abiff - a fictional entity that was responsible for gifting
      Solomon with the wisdom to build the first temple (833 BCE)

HUMAN

To be human is to care.
To be human is to share.
To be human is to learn how to keep the ego
      locked up in its lair.
To be human is to accept error.
To be human is to stand up for what you believe in
      and proudly jab your fist into the air.

To be human is to be conscious.
To expand one's consciousness,
      one must be aware.
      To be human is to accept.
      Accept that life will not always be fair.

To be human is to be humble.
Be more than just human.
Be the lightning strike
      after the thunder rumbles!

FACELESS

Faceless as am I,
disguised as a man
        amongst a garden of lies,
for thy will only ever have one eye.
        I am nobody.
I am everywhere
        and I am everything.

What am I?

I am Ether.
        I have no body.
I am limitless.
        There is no bottom.
I have no end.

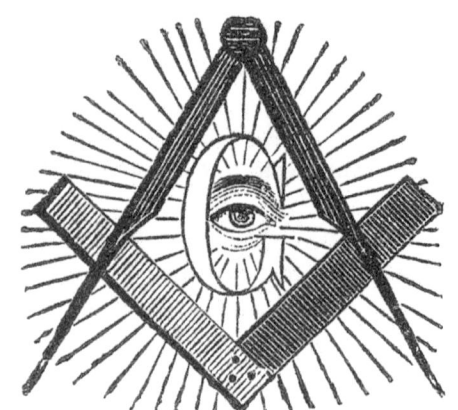

OUROBOROS

I am just a seeker.
        In my search I have found.
My discovery was so profound,
        I fell face first into the ground.
I could not tell up from down.

I am no fool,
but I portrayed myself as a clown.
        Chasing my tail in circles,
eternally, I will keep going round and around.
        No longer do I live in silence.
I have finally made a sound!

For the Emerald Tablets that lie in the roots are
buried in the ground.
Never will they rot – eternally waiting to be found.

Ether - the clear sky; the upper regions of air beyond the clouds.
Ouroboros - a symbol of a serpent chasing its tail
        to symbolize infinite rebirth and renewal of the soul.

SERPENTINE

Steady as she goes
just a whistle in the wind as it blows.

Her luminescence was nothing short of a glow.

How did something come from nothing?
No one truly knows.

The mountain top explodes
as her river of lava flows.
Even the valley bottom on a sunny day
still has its lows.

To choose is to have chose.
An anchor will always have its bows.
If I am only a tree, then her roots are my toes.
The ravens will always sing in harmony amongst
the croak of the crows!

RAVEN CONSPIRACY

The raven would lark at the stark
as its song should mesmerize me.
Over the mountains and into the valleys,
I am in Love with the reflection of the light blue sea.
If life is only a tree
and in its roots lie the key,
suddenly it is then that I see:

"The universe is bigger than you, bigger than me,
bigger than he, bigger than she.
United we stand, together as One —
interconnected and collectively!
The guardians will always stand on guard for thee —
never in pairs, always in threes,
from then until now, from now until eternity.
What if all they needed was a prophet to fulfill the prophecy?
I guess it would only take a mad cow to set the rest of the sheep free!
If all there ever was is all there could ever be,
how did you become you, and how did I become me?"

MOONLIT MIRROR

Oh sister moon,
       I did not mean to let you down.
My time came a little bit too soon.
To the darkness,
I have now become immune.
       My soul is as ancient as the Germanic rune.
Love is the light.

(so I presume)

In an absence of matter,
       a ray will still shine bright
in a vacuum of silence sealed ever so tight.

I have now ascended.
       My consciousness has taken flight.
Victory now is the only thing I have in sight.
       Teach me wrong from right.
Only now it is the internal fire that I have to fight.

Say goodnight to the twilight.
       Next time I must use all of my might.
Stuck in the cold depths of darkness,
       I must make it past the frost bite.

Does it make a sound when the celestial spark ignites?

Very soon we will all unite
       under the warm luminescent glow of the moonlight.

Funny thing is, I am so hungry
       but I have lost my appetite,
for now is the time to fight –
       fight for the human right!

Germanic - vikings.
Rune- ancient alphabets carved into stone.

MONAD

There are different levels of meditation.
Part of the craft is learning how to tolerate patience
      and leave no reservations.
The combination of X+Y
      zEquals my concentration.

No more hesitation.
      Infinite Light is my emancipation.
May Love be the only proclamation.

Attainment is enlightenment
      through trivium and quadrivium.
Now that I am finally starting to understand,
      no longer do I wish to be the man.
Great Architect of the Universe,
      please just teach me from the altar as it stands.

Em ancipation - freedom: the liberation of Infinite Beauty.
Proclamation - sacred promise.
Trivium (Latin) - logic, grammar, and rhetoric.
Quadrivium (Latin) - arithmetic, music, geometry, astronomy.
Altar (Archaic) - symbolism of the alignment between the celestial equator and the source and creation of all light (human vs. cosmos). It was later adopted by some religious organizations as a place to preform blood sacrifice (light vs. darkness).

NON NOBIS SOLUM

Rise up my Love for lo,
    the long winter has passed.
The rain is over and gone.
    The flowers appear on Earth.
The time of the singing birds has come,
    and the voice of the turtle can be heard in our land.

If you want to find my treasure it's carved in the rocks,
    it lies in the roots,
        it is buried in the sand.

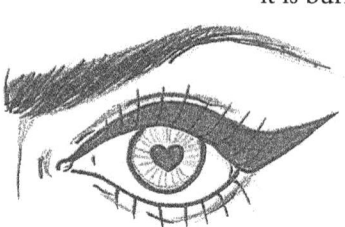

ALPHA OMEGA

What if
Ω a long time ago Ω
in a galaxy far, far away,
there once was a Goddess named Alpha
and a God named Omega?
Their children, Sonic and Sega, used to play a game.
Although back then, it was not called
"Fortune and Fame."
It was called,
"Who Can Keep the Flame?"
The catch was there was only one fire pit.
The keeper of the flame is named victor,
and they shall get to write their own script
while the rest of the scrolls are to be ripped.
What if shapes could move,
possibly even shift?
We all have the celestial gift.
Just allow your spirit to uplift.
Dive into the ocean abyss
because you are the golden rift!

ODE TO GEOMETRY

I am me.
      I can be
      a kaleidoscope.
There is no end to this rope.
      Time may only be just a slick joke.
All I have left is hope.

360th degree,
      the better human is all I achieve to be.
Faceless as I am,
      thine name starts with a capital G.

The seer that I am,
      now that I have seen,
enlightened by the light
      I have discovered my aura is green.
Sometimes nothing is as it seems.
      Am I lucid or is this a dream?

Sweet bitterness is the darkness of night.
      I am alright
so long as the moon is shining bright.

No longer will I be
      as bitter as the salty sea.
I have the laws of reflection down to a T.
      Euclid and Pythagoras taught thee
the simplicity of sacred geometry.

Aristotle speculated that
      X+Y shall always equal Z.

(geocentrically)

The most important amalgam
      is A squared minus C
will always equal B.

Euclid's 47th problem solved me!
Geocentrically – 'centra of the universe
Centra –the body of the spine that holds the arches of the 33 columns in human anatomy.

SO BELOW

As so,
I stare into the darkness below
from the heaven's abode.
We must always look upward and onwards
if the light is as above.

Not like an eagle,
I am an angel.
I
flap my wings as a dove.

GLOW

Oh, the crystal of the morning dew,
    I drink from her fountain of youth
    as I am drunk by the celestial stew.
She is made by the moon.
She is at the end of the rainbow past the scarlet skies of doom.
She is the Goddess laughing off into Infinity and beyond
    while riding a golden broom.
    Her grey skies will always have a beautiful bloom!

Only in the ether could tomorrow never come too soon.
    Over and out, through and through.
Broadened are the lights that light up my horizons.
    May this world also be anew.

AQUA

You are the flower that when I died
    I chose to be laid beside.
The disguise of an empty vessel is where I used to reside.
As fluid as we are, we will always be a slave to your tides.
A gent. of a groom will always need a beaut. of a bride
    in order for the New World to survive.
Oh Annie, are we riding the bull
    or just along for the ride?

Only once I stare into the sun do I realize I cannot undo all that has been undone.

INFINITE EXPANSION FOUNDATION

"To provide a safe place for self-expression for at-risk youth, we aim to inspire creativity and promote self-awareness through Art Therapy, mindfulness, and mentorship of youth through structured workshops and programs in a youth-run center, open to any and all youth, as all youth these days are at-risk."

Liberal Arts Mentorship Program

Our Vision

Introduction

It is our intention to start a Liberal Arts Mentorship Program for at–risk youth. Our goal is to provide a safe space for the youth to socialize after school through creative means such as art, music, poetry, yoga, and with the opportunity to pursue further development in Liberal Arts. At Infinite Expansion Foundation, we realized from our personal experiences that the ability to express yourself creatively is fundamental in the development of self-awareness and self-love. Our goal is to provide the youth with the necessary tools in order for them to be able to express themselves with the help of mentors to guide students in the right direction to help set and reach their goals. Mentors will also assist with tutoring and homework. We hope to encourage students to embrace, pursue, and develop artistic and social skills.

As a result of an identity crisis and through our personal experiences, we have concluded that society as a whole has lost sense of the importance of getting in touch with one's creative side. We believe in the importance of Liberal Arts as it can help an individual grow and learn to love oneself respectfully. Our goal is to not only provide a place of expression, but also a place to spark intellectual conversations. Calls will be made to local artists and those knowledgeable in these creative fields to volunteer their time and share their experience. It is our intention to start a Liberal Arts Mentorship Program in British Columbia, Canada. We are asking for your financial support to help us raise our initial goal of **$1.3 million dollars** to help get this pilot project operational.

Program Purpose and Objectives

Goals:

- Prevent addiction and reduce crime and violence through self-expression, education, and inspiration.
- Inspire creativity amongst youth and coach self-taught techniques.
- Develop and improve interpersonal/intrapersonal communication skills.
- Provide a safe space for expression and learning.
- Help students with homework and promote self-discovery.
- Provide an individualized aspect of learning: "What would you like to learn about today?"
- Inspire intellectual conversations to further their quest for knowledge.
- Provide positive role models to allow our students to achieve their goals and become productive members of society.
- Provide the tools needed for self-discovery and self-expression to allow the youth to create their own reality.
- Develop inspiration through visualization.
- Increase individual cognitive consonance.

Objectives:

Our goal is to create a safe space for the youth to inspire creativity and develop a quest for knowledge in an effort to prevent drug addiction and take action against the opioid epidemic. We aim to help the youth who are at-risk for addiction and teach them how to be productive members of society while helping those suffering from an identity crisis. At Infinite Expansion Foundation, we believe Art Therapy is part of the solution.

Our concept includes the following:
A quiet section on one floor with an open space with easels, canvases, carving and pottery equipment. This floor will also contain a library with books from various philosophers, poets, historians, visionary authors and artists, half a dozen computers, and desks for homework. We plan on turning the other floor into the "loud section." This will consist of an area for students who wish to play music, dance, and practice musical instruments. There will be a small recording studio and a computer with mixing capabilities and software production.

We would like to provide an individualized aspect of learning with certain days dedicated to professionally guided workshops such as creative writing, yoga, meditation, painting, carving, graphic design, and musically inclined lessons.

Target & Activities

Our vision is to create a space free from judgment with the necessary tools to allow kids to find their own methods of self-expression. It is going to be a collaboration of intellectuals, artisans, and mentors with hands on experiences coming together to share their knowledge in order to inspire students to find healthy activities and hobbies to supplement addictive and destructive behaviors.

Our vision to have a facility that will contain the following:
- Arts and craft room: paint, canvases, easels, carving tools, and pottery wheels.
- Music room: musical instruments and a basic recording studio for aspiring artists.
- Library/poetry room.
- Computers and desks for studying and mentorship.
- One-on-one counseling with students to help set goals and plans to reach their goals.
- Tutorship and mentorship of high school students.
- A magnetic board with educational and beautiful magnetic words written to inspire creativity.

Not only do we want to provide a place for learning and expression, once established, we hope to host various workshops to teach basic job and life skills. This mentorship program will potentially lead to an employment program incorporated into our daily activities.

The impact on the community could include:
- The prevention of addiction and crime.
- Improve interpersonal communication amongst youth in order to help them excel in school.
- Improve intrapersonal skills to help students create and reach their goals through insight.

Addiction, crime, and violence go hand in hand. Any youth is at-risk of becoming a victim of drug addiction. The overall benefit this program will have on the community could include:
- Lower rates of property crime.
- Reduction of overdoses on a yearly basis.
- Increase the rates of students graduating high school.

We will help students become aware of their strengths and weaknesses to leverage their strengths while reducing the impact of their weaknesses. Teaching self-worth will lead them to a better understanding of their place in society so they can use their creativity to pursue a career they will love.

Proof of Concept in Regards to Art Therapy

With the fentanyl crisis growing more and more rampant each year, action must be taken to help our youth and provide a safe space for them. The youth is our future.

Every year that goes by, the number of homelessness amongst the youth grows exponentially and is becoming a real crisis in our society. We feel that our mentorship program will give them senses of purpose to help them better understand their role in society.

It is our belief that addiction can lead to homelessness, crime and possible violence. Art Therapy may have a profound effect on preventing addiction and crime.

Art Therapy is a great way to deal with past traumas and also to release aggression through expression. Here is part of an article titled "Physiological Benefits of Art Therapy" written by Asa Dawn Brown, in 2012 regarding the potential benefits of art therapy.

https://www.ccpa-accp.ca/psychological-benefits-of-art-therapy/

- Art Therapy is capable of promoting self-expression, feelings, and emotions.
- It has an ability to facilitate positive perspectives on one's self. It is capable of promoting a sense of personal independence, self-reliance, and self-sufficiency.
- Art Therapy has an ability to help a child work through difficult experiences. It allows a child to verbally and nonverbally communicate emotions that might otherwise be abandoned or sealed from society. Therapy instills constructive techniques to self-manage.
- It can increase one's awareness and orientation (i.e. persons, places, dates, and times). It is capable of facilitating and developing strategies for hand-eye coordination, fine and gross motor skills, and finger dexterity and speed.
- It encourages the development of healthy coping strategies.
- Therapy can facilitate insight, empathy, and acceptance of other's life challenges.
- It is capable of promoting problem-solving skills.
- Art therapy is capable of exploring, managing, and providing insight into traumatic experiences.
- A child receiving therapy is encouraged to develop interpersonal skills. It empowers and gives a voice to those receiving therapy. It is capable of helping a child increase their attention span, while decreasing any festering frustrations.

"Art therapy is a mental health profession that uses the creative process of art making to improve and enhance the physical, mental and emotional well-being of individuals of all ages." (American Art Therapy Association, 2012, Online)

"Numerous case studies have reported that art therapy benefits patients with both emotional and physical illnesses. Case studies have involved many areas, including burn recovery in adolescents and young children, eating disorders, emotional impairment in young children, reading performance, and childhood grief. Studies of adults using art therapy have included adults or families in bereavement, patients and family members dealing with addictions. Some of the potential uses of art therapy to be researched include reducing anxiety levels, improving recovery times, decreasing hospital stays, improving communication and social function, and pain control." (American Cancer Society, 2012, Online)

"Over the course of the year, the number of young people who spend some time homeless in Canada is as many as 40,000, and on any given night, there may be up to 7,000 homeless youth." — https://www.covenanthousetoronto.ca/homeless-youth/Youth-Homelessness [1]

Here is a passage written by **Graeme Martell** expressing how art changed his life, *"I feel that embracing not only art, but the liberal arts is fundamental in helping people understand the beauty in not only the world around them, but also their purpose in this universe. After learning to express thyself only then did I finally get to know myself, and in turn, Love myself for whom I am. The quest of expression to see the beauty in myself has led me to see the beauty in nature and also other individuals. Through self-expression, I have learned to respect other people's opinions and beliefs. The first lost art that I discovered was painting. One day I had an overwhelming need to express myself, so I created a painting from drywall with various black and white paint I had lying around my house. Recently, I have discovered philosophy and have been writing allegorical poems that have a deeper sense of self-reflection. It has led me to* **supplement my chemical addictions into an addiction of expression and knowledge** *to learn, and to create. Poetry has allowed me to view things from a completely different perspective. For example, here is a poem I wrote* **'If we were to think of ourselves as a plant, and its flowers are to symbolize Love, then only after we have harnessed the power from the sun, could we grow and bloom. Our seeds of Love will be spread by the winds of change.'** *The discovery of art has made me the person I am today."*

Summary

Thank you for taking the time to read our proposal. We are interested in pursuing potential partnerships. This pilot project will hopefully be the start of something much bigger. Together, we can make the world a brighter and more beautiful place! It is our belief that inspiring creativity will lead to the creation of a brighter and more beautiful world. Our mission statement is, **"*An Infinite Expansion of Infinite Possibilities, an Infinite Idea of Infinite Logic and Infinite Reason*"** Simply said, we are focused and truly believe anything is possible. We believe that knowledge is the contemplation of the individual, while wisdom is the collaboration from the minds of many. Financially, any nominal donation will help in our efforts to reach our goal of **$1.3 million dollars.** We greatly appreciate your support. If you are not in a financial position to help, we are also looking for volunteers.

Illuminated Age of Aquarius

I'm sure at some point in all of our lives, one of our parents has told us, "Do what you're told and don't ask questions." I say it's now time to question everything as we enter the "New Age of Aquarius." (The Age of Enlightenment - An Eternal Equinox of Internal Light) Humanity could in the next 2,160 years finally see a shift of universal consciousness. But what does it mean to pull the veil off of the ancient disguise? It means it is time to question everything — think outside the box, be creative, live to create. Love thyself and love all. Do not only be One with thyself, also be One with "All that is everything."— Thoth.

In order to see the beauty in our existence, what if we only need to open our third eye, also known as our Ethereal Eye? Maybe color is just an illusion, and what we perceive to be color may just be modulated refractions of wavelengths from the rays of the sun. If true, this would mean that there is only light. Although it is invisible, we can only see its reflection! Darkness is only shadow, with both making half of the whole. Together they are Infinite, but they are also all that is definite. Would it make any sense if the only thing that is definite is also Infinite? The space between the known and the unknown is known as dark matter. If this were true, would that mean the ambiguity of clarity is dependent upon the resolution of abstract illusion?

I will now try to explain my logic behind the phrase you just read. Ambiguity can be defined as follows: open-mindedness, nothing is exact, or finite; consciousness is infinite. Clarity for the most part explains itself; it can also be referred to the transparency of Enlightenment. Enlightenment can be seen as looking at life through a kaleidoscope rather than a magnifying glass. In the phrase "resolution of abstract illusion," abstract can be referred to its exact definition as: *"existing in thought or as an idea but not having a physical or concrete existence"* — *Oxford Dictionary.* In regards to illusion, I will also use its exact definition as reference: *"a thing that is or is likely to be wrongly perceived or interpreted by the senses."* — *Oxford Dictionary.* Therefore, what I am trying to say is that just because our 5 senses cannot perceive it to be real, the reality of life is only as real as your consciousness believes it to be. If existence merely means to exist, then I believe we should all exist unanimously in harmony. I'm hoping in this so called meaningless life, that you are starting to search for meaning, whatever that means.

Alchemy is now universally defined as the study of the relationship between consciousness and matter. The archaic definition is the ability to produce the Elixir of Life (fictional concoction that allows you to talk to God). The Elixir also, hypothetically, can create a universal menstruum (alkahest) capable of dissolving even gold. With mercuric acid, this can theoretically trans-mutate lead into gold. The translation of alchemy can be broken down into two clauses: (Al) which is Arabic meaning "origin", and "chemy" which has been derived from the ancient Egyptian word "kemet" meaning beloved land or black land. The translation black land can loosely stipulate notions of black magic, but it is quite the opposite.

Thoth, the Ultimate God of Knowledge and Wisdom once stated "As above, so below." This statement can be referred to as the relationship between the light of the heavens and the darkness, or shadow cast upon Earth. Also remember that the color black absorbs more energy than any other color. That's why it's not a good idea to wear black on a warm day — or is it?

The heavens are referred to as the light. It is believed that heaven also exists in the mind. The darkness or blackness is referred to as the earth due to its dependence from the sun to sustain life. Consciousness is the light; the physical or material body is darkness. Symbiotically speaking, for all species and organisms on Earth we need light from the sun in order for growth; we also need warmth from the sun in order to survive. The sun is above our heads, therefore the heavens are referred to as the "above" in, "As above, so below." The light from the sun is the light from the heavens that illuminate the darkness. The "below" is the intrinsic relationship seen from the eyes of the earth, staring into the rays of the heaven's abode. This is known as the symbiotic relationship between all matter that interconnect us all in a singularity.

Although I am One, I am only half of a human, and it is in the black land where I will stand as I drag my toes; I will draw lines in the sand.

Half of a man meaning I am made up of two parts: the physical and the metaphysical. Man not as in male but as in Hu(Man): entity vs. aether.

The trigonometry of alchemy categorizes the breakdown of all elements into three categories — an allegory of a trinity to symbolize infinity. The top of the pyramid would be known as "Sulfur" or the "Soul" symbolized as oil. The mind is referred to as "Mercury"; it is symbolized as spirit or alcohol. The physical body is referred to as "Salt" or a "Crystal." All three of these compounds are inert and will not spoil or decay. Although alcohol can dissipate, it will not break down without an induction of heat.

Aethereal can be broken down into A-Ether; A as in "Alpha", known as the beginning. The Archaic definition of Ether is *"a very rarefied and highly elastic substance formerly believed to permeate all space, including the interstices between the particles of matter, and to be the medium whose vibrations constituted light and other electromagnetic radiation"* — Oxford Dictionary. Ether can be referred to as the 5Th element. The literary definition of Ether is *"the clear sky; the upper regions of air beyond the clouds"* — Oxford Dictionary. (See Figure 3)

As Infinite as am I, I am only as finite as the clouds in the sky.

The realms of the divine are known as the Etheric Plains or the Halls of Amenti. The Halls of Amenti are allegory referring to the attainment of enlightenment. It most definitely is not a portal to the underworld. To be enlightened is to be illuminated. You are illuminated once you enter the internal matrix of eternal knowledge passed down from your ancestors, known as, "The Ancient Ones" Awakened and alive, gifted with Infinite Light, you now become a dweller of life. The fire in your soul transcends into a flower of Infinite Light and Love.

"Not desired I, but the attainment of wisdom." — Thoth Emerald tablet #2 (trans. by Doreal)

Thoth is known in Egyptian or Sumerian mythology as the son of Ea (Enki). Ea is known as the eldest son of Annu and Mannu, the primordial Father and Mother of all that is everything. Thoth is also known in Greek mythology as Hermes. Thoth was an alchemist who created what's known to scholars and anthropologists as the Emerald Tablets. The Emerald Tablets have been scribed out of alchemically trans-mutated emerald and are completely inert.

The entropic decay of dark matter does not affect them. This violates the second law of thermodynamics because the molecules that the tablets are constructed of do not vibrate; they are completely still. It has confused many scientists because as of today, this process cannot be replicated. The tablets are 36,000 years old and are thought to contain words of wisdom from the ancient gods pertaining to the spiritual or divine realm of our existence. It reveals the lost word spoken in Atlantis. It is the key for the seeker to end its search for meaning and to explain the unexplainable. The intellectual or creative thinker builds their own bridge between the material and the immaterial. A rhetorical question has an obvious answer. A philosophical question has no definite answer — only your answer. Ask yourself questions without answers.

Symbolically speaking, this divine knowledge can be referred to as Serpent knowledge. Ancient symbology is the key to unlocking our understanding of the cosmos and the invisible plains of existence that surround us. When we look at the caduceus — known to us in modern day as the universal medical symbol — we see the staff of Hermes with two serpents entwined around it. If it is said to be a fictional object, then how did it become such a prominent figure in society?

The significance of symbolism and sacred numerology and geometry is revealed in the cosmos.

The study of the cosmos was a very important aspect of ancient civilizations. Its importance has been lost in the world we live in today. To open your eyes to the truth is to question everything, even the light. Symbols are hidden in plain sight. Once we uncover their purpose, only then does it help us with our understanding of life. Symbols when deciphered help explain our vast diverse history that has been lost, hidden, and/or destroyed through crusades, war and conquest. If greed and war were simply nonexistent, then we could focus on what's really important: creating a beautiful future for our children, saving the planet, and the discovery of thyself. The quest of beauty can only be seen through the eye of the beholder. Maybe the only meaning of life is to search for meaning as long as it means something to you.

Globally and collectively, in order to effectively draft ergonomic solutions to combat global warming, hunger, and addiction we must get creative. Alchemy, if widely studied and accepted amongst scholars and scientists and viewed as plausible, could possibly bridge the gap between consciousness and matter. Human vs. Nature — to coexist with nature and live in harmony, we must respect Mother Earth and appreciate the Father Sun. Respect can also be defined as equality. We must treat her as an equal to him while we evolve. Evolution not only in regards to technological advancements but also collectively. As Mother Earth pleads and begs for her life, may we stand together united as One to save her from the rape of her resources and pollution of her land. Find a way to help and do your part!

The last hope of saving humanity is to open up our consciousness to the shift in energy that is happening in Aquarius. As we leave Pisces known as the Dark Age and enter the Golden Age of Aquarius, the shift in energy is believed to allow one's consciousness to be so clear, it could be seen as clairvoyance. If you are wondering how to attain enlightenment, there is no definite set of directions. It is a lifestyle change with an inverted outlook of reality. Universal knowledge is attained through exercise, meditation, mindfulness and self-discipline.

The power of breath let the living dead unrest.

If we spend our whole lives rushing from one event to the next, then we will always be trying to save time. We will be glued to our technologies and we will forever lose sight of the natural beauty in everything that exists everywhere. What if time is only a ruler to measure the relationship between each day that passes on Earth in relation the Cosmos. Does time change or do we change in time? The Ancient Ones understood the significance and impact that the cosmos and zodiacs played in one's self-work as well as universally. There are 12 months in a year and 12 cycles in the cosmic cycle known as the Zodiac (or are there 13?). It is estimated that the cycle of the Zodiac lasts 25,920 years. Planets are also thought to represent different chakras or energies that lie within. There are 7 chakras contained in our physical existence and 5 etheric chakras which are an extension of one's consciousness visualized in the invisible plains of existence (imagination). Is it a coincidence that they also equal 12? In Greek and Sumerian mythology, told through hieroglyphs and pictographs, it also states that there are "Twelve Great Gods" — Sitchin.

In Sumerian mythology they are: Timat, Enlil, Enki or Ea, Marduk, Ishtar, Sin, Utu, Nisaba, Ashur, Ninkasi, — all of whom were descendants of the Primordial father Annu and primordial mother Nammu. The bible also states there are 12 tribes.

It is my hope in the Age of Aquarius that we can further understand and study the divine Etheric plains. In our studies, may we find solutions to problems that put the fate of humanity at risk. May we once again see the beauty in everything so we can build a bridge to a brighter and a more peaceful future.

If a sheep is to symbolize ignorance and conformity to the norm of reality, then in this Age of Enlightenment may all the sheep awaken and become shepherds — the masters of their own destinies. If a lamb is to symbolize innocence, then in the Golden Age may they grow into shepherds capable of setting all of the rest of the sheep free. There are only two types of shepherds: those who raise sheep to slaughter and those who raise sheep to keep their bloodline alive. In the fields will they forever graze freely.

Beauty Is Universal

In a conquest for money and meaningless materialistic possessions, the universe as a whole has lost its concept of liberalism. Liberalism was the very just and great ideal that gave birth to the democracy we live in today. A direct consequence from the loss of individualism was the corruption of liberalism. By putting the needs of, "Thy powers vested in thee" ahead of the needs of the commonwealth, this has lead us into a reality that the elite have effectively created for us. The people have lost their voice due to corporate domination. Superpowers have effectively branded our lives. The universe is losing sense for not only the need, but also the importance of embracing the ancient Liberal Arts. Philosophy is quickly becoming a lost art. All cultures seem to be disintegrating faster and faster.

The universal idea of individualism is to put the needs of the people ahead of the pursuit of profit. Throughout the universe, the quest for self-worth is now thought to be attained through the purchase of expensive and luxurious items (material attainment). Most of these possessions are in fact unpractical and useless. If we are too focused on the quest of self-importance, we lose sight of the need for the quest of beauty. Self-discovery leads to discovery of the abilities that lie within oneself to create art, music, motion and poetry. Together, the quest for beauty and the discovery in thyself will lead to an awareness of self-worth. We shouldn't forget that reality is in the eye of the beholder. As Abraham Lincoln once said,

"You are only as happy as you make up your mind to be."

Our purpose in life needs to be a quest to see the beauty in ourselves and everything in our co-existence rather than social status. It was quadrivium (arts, arithmetic, astronomy, and geometry) and trivium (grammar, rhetoric, and logic) that led us into the Renaissance. It will be the conquest for beauty that will save us! Ask yourself what does beauty mean to you? If nature was only a mere reflection of true beauty, then you must also be a mirror of nature. Beauty is where the mountains meet the sky and where the water meets the land, as well as it is the children playing in the sand. It is everywhere and it is all around us but we are blinded by chaos. To find sense in all the nonsense is senseless. Does this make any sense to you?

If beauty paves the road for love, and love in its purest form is happiness, why are we so concerned with illusions of grandeur in the form of self-importance?

Theosophy and philosophy go hand in hand. Philosophy is the expression and study of knowledge, reason, and values regarding our existence in the universe.

"We can easily forgive a child who is afraid of the dark; the real tragedy of life is when men are afraid of the light" — *Plato*

Theosophy is the study of one's soul, the divine and their purpose in the universe.

"Before the soul can see, the harmony within must be attained, and fleshly eyes be rendered to an illusion" — *Helena Petrovna Blavatsky.*

"The universe is worked and guided from within outwards." — *Helena Petronova Blavatsky.*

It is quotes like these that make you question everything. They lead to a desire to think for yourself and relearn forgotten universal knowledge. If taught unbiasedly, Language Arts can help us to design a future in which we would want our children to live in. By inspiring people to think about their existence and contemplate on one's purpose, together we shall all collaborate to better understand this universe! If we are to form our own opinions and formulate our own individual beliefs, then we will have the ability to create our own reality. We need to look to our ancestors for guidance as they once lived in harmony with nature as well as each other.

History taught in schools today is but a mere fractal of a piece of the puzzle. In school, we learn very little about art and philosophy. Pythagoras is viewed by most as a mathematician rather than a philosopher. Most people have never heard of Helena Blavatsky or the <u>Secret</u>

<u>Doctrine.</u> Reference upon the "Legend of Etana" or the "Epic of Gilgamesh" is not mentioned nor made part of modern curriculum purposely. Philosophy and theosophy inspired creativity, that in turn gave birth to the Renaissance. The Renaissance was the blueprint which built the reality we live in today.

A quest for knowledge gave birth to democracy. We live in a so called just and free country where everything costs money. We are losing touch with our identity as well as our culture. Our lives have been made so easy, we are effectively forgetting how to think for ourselves! If to remember is to mean that we shall never forget, then we shall remember that we once shifted from a medieval oligarchical feudal way of life to a new linear perspective of reality. Today we know this as universal freedom, meaning our ancestors created the world they wanted their children to live in! Our ancestors created this New World by embracing the Liberal Arts. Freedom of thought and expression led us to the desire for knowledge, equality, and justice. This became the basis of the Constitution and the Charter of Rights and Freedoms in Canada. When society opened their eyes and unified, the commonwealth then demanded freedom over fiefdom.

All of them said to the King and the Queen, "We have had enough. We want a voice." Change then became a reality. Equality was shaped from freedom of thought, freedom of speech, and freedom of expression.

Universal Freedom was shaped by wisdom. Wisdom is a result of strength, unity and collaboration of individual knowledge. Only then, can we finally see the beauty in everything. For example, when we look at the architecture of ancient structures and also historical buildings, we see the beauty engrained in their design. Not only do we notice they are beautiful, but are ergonomically designed with a sense of purpose in mind. Would you rather live in a concrete jungle or a garden of stones?

We cannot blame anyone but ourselves for allowing this tyranny and treachery to shape the world we live in today. By wearing their logos on our chest, we effectively provide them with free advertising. In turn, this gives them domination and control over the Free Market. They set their own trends and expect you to follow them if you want to be noticed. For the longest time, I was afraid to express myself. Only after expressing thyself did I finally get to meet myself. After I got to know myself, I learned to love myself for whom I AM. It was then that I learned to respect others for who they are. If change is our last hope for the universe, then we must evolve or die.

If you are more financially capable than others, I beg you for the sake of humanity to ask yourself, "Why do I really need 11 flamboyant sports cars, and this $9,000 white designer hat?" Flashing its logos all over creates a universal image to symbolize wealth and privilege. Why do we have a need to show people we have more money than they do? Does this make us feel better about ourselves?

To feel better about myself I wake up every day asking myself, "How can I make the world a better place? What can I learn today? How can I help others?" I challenge you to do the same. May my only legacy be the positive impact I have had on other people's lives.

Stand tall! Speak out! Stand together! Be who you are! Do what you love! And you will inspire! If we do not create a green, sufficient, sustainable future of harmony, unity, and universal peace, we will forever be history.

Liberalism: political doctrine that takes protecting and enhancing the freedom of the individual to be the central problem of politics. Liberals typically believe that government is necessary to protect individuals from being harmed by others, but they also recognize that government itself can pose a threat to liberty. — Wikipedia

Individualism: the moral stance, political philosophy, ideology, or social outlook that emphasizes the moral worth of the individual Individualists promote the exercise of one's goals and desires and so value independence and self-reliance and advocate that interests of the individual should achieve precedence over the state or a social group, while opposing external interference upon one's own interests by society or institutions such as the government. Individualism is often defined in contrast to totalitarianism, collectivism, and more corporate social forms. — Wikipedia

The bumble of the bee is as the flower is of me.

"Beehive"
William M. Cunningham
1874

About the Author

Graeme Patrick Martell is the ideal author of a book whose thoughtful content considers such subjects as illicit danger, lucid dreaming, enlightened understandings, and the constant and marvelous powers of energy. He has been a drug user, has been stuck down the rabbit hole, and is a transformed graduate of the School of Life. With this collection, he hopes to help others find the light.

After six years being addicted to fentanyl, Martell gained his sobriety through a range of healthy means of expression, including painting, poetry, and skateboarding. He also became a volunteer fire fighter in Logan Lake and volunteers his spare time helping Infinite Expansion Foundation, a non-profit organization based in Langley, BC, that is dedicated to making the world a happier and more beautiful place, with a focus on helping those who suffer from addiction and mental illness, including at-risk youth.

Equinox is the result of Martell's decision to write a book as a fundraiser in support of the foundation's Liberal Arts Mentorship Program. He lives in Cascadia, Pacific Northwest.

Guide to Abstract:

Trace your thoughts from their origin; allowing the colors, if at all existent, to reflect only your emotions. Allow the sound to guide you through your thoughts, release. Release all tension as you let your thoughts flow freely through your hand and into your creation. Focus on how the instrument feels as it leaves a trail on your canvas. The mark its makes is a mark of yours. The beauty of creation results in art. You are an artist, you are beautiful, go ahead and create. Admire your own creation; do not try to define it, for it is what it is. Whatever you see it for, is only seen through your eyes. Let the abstract of the unknown that reveals itself in your design form its own shape; do not try to shape it. Imagine that you are as vast as the water, but remember to take into account that you are still only a droplet. Now that you are as still water droplet, imagine the shape you will take from the vibrations of the music as they pass through your firmament. Are they symmetrical spirals, geometrical gradients, or do they even possibly mirror a kaleidoscope?

You are the energy holding together the bonds of your water droplet; there is no need to imagine, as the image is of you. The crystalline covalent bonds that hold you together are illuminated through the song of the sounds. Notice this light. Embrace this light. Let it transpire as you become this light. Do not search for this light; simply visualize it until you can feel the warmth emanating from the light you see shining from within.